Remembering Georgy

Remembering Georgy

LETTERS FROM THE HOUSE OF IZIEU

BY SERGE KLARSFELD

Aperture

THIS PUBLICATION HAS BEEN MADE POSSIBLE
BY THE GENEROUS SUPPORT OF ELIANE AND TOMMASO ZANZOTTO
AND DOROTHY S. AND MYRON B. HOFFMAN

FORTY-FIVE YEARS OF SUFFERING
THE LOSS OF ONE'S ONLY CHILD...

Georgy, Georg Halpern, was one of the forty-four children who resided at the children's home in Izieu, one of the many Jewish orphanages established throughout France to house children whose parents had been deported or who were in hiding during the Holocaust. Not one of the children survived. Forty-two of them were assassinated by the Nazis in Auschwitz-Birkenau. The other two children, the oldest ones, were murdered by the S.S. in a forest in Estonia, near Tallin. Their principal, Miron Zlatin, suffered the same fate. They were all put to death because of racial hatred, because they were born Jewish.

Of the seven members of the staff at Izieu, the "Colony of the Refugee Children of the Hérault," only one instructor, Léa Feldblum, was still alive in 1945.

Her voice was heard at the trial of Klaus Barbie, the executioner of the children of Izieu who was guilty of the round-up of April 6, 1944 that ended these young lives. After her testimony she fell silent, as did, Ita-Rosa Halaunbrenner and Fortunée Benguigui, the "Mothers of Courage," the heroic and martyred mothers of the children of Izieu. They had joined my wife, Beate, and I in Munich and La Paz in 1971 and 1972, when we thwarted Barbie's impunity, when we found him and

unmasked him. It took us ten more years to succeed in bringing Barbie to trial at the place of his crimes. And it was there that the mothers gave their testimonies. Thereafter, Sabine Zlatin, the founder of the House of Izieu, was heard once more. Before her death in 1996, she succeeded in recreating a new House of Izieu, a House of Remembrance where the memory of the forty-four children is alive and well. The nation of France and the President of the Republic, François Mitterand, actively participated in this resurrection.

In 1984, following a long and worldwide investigation, I published *The Children of Izieu*. This work reconstructed the painful life of each child. It was the first time this was accomplished and has served as a reference for subsequent books.

In Lyon in 1987, I pleaded the case for each of these children who are so close to me that they inspired me to establish the "The Memorial of the Jewish Children deported from France." As if the House of Izieu were the size of France, I tried to do with 11,000 children what I was able to do with forty-four: to commemorate the lives so cruelly cut short by the insanity of anti-Semitism; to help them come through this history not as objects thereof but as individuals.

I continued to scrupulously collect every bit of information concerning each of the forty-four children of Izieu. In February 1997, thanks to the dedication of Eliane Rawicz-Zanzotto and her husband Tommaso, I was able to acquire Georgy Halpern's relics, which had been preserved by his parents, Julius and Sérafine, until their deaths.

Julius Halpern, a dentist, son of Abraham and Rosa, was born in Lemberg, Poland, on June 6, 1905. His wife, Sérafine Friedmann, daughter of Ignaz and Sarolta, was born in Vienna on September 23, 1907. They were married on August 18, 1929 in Vienna where they made their home at 29 Rotenturmstrasse.

Georgy, their only child, was born in Vienna on October 30, 1935. After the Anschluss, when Germany annexed Austria, the Halpern family took refuge in France. There, they were subjected to the security measures taken by the government against German and Austrian nationals after the war had been declared; these measures were heightened after the German army invaded Belgium in May 1940. Having fallen ill, Sérafine was admitted to the St. Louis Hospital in Perpignan and later to the Espérance Sanatorium in Hauteville (Ain). Meanwhile, Julius was brought into a unit of foreign laborers. As for Georgy, he was entrusted to the O.S.E. (Oeuvre de Secours aux Enfants: Society for the Protection of Children) and spent a long time at the Children's Home in Chaumont (Creuse) and later at the Château de Masgelier in the same administrative department. (I myself was a boarder there; Georgy was forty-three days younger than I.) He then went to the House of Champestre in Lodève (Hérault), before going to the House of Izieu (Ain), via Montpellier at the end of April 1943. This home was located in the Italian occupied zone where Jews had felt safe. Danger resurfaced when the Germans invaded the Italian zone in September 1943, and on April 6, 1944 catastrophe struck the House of Izieu.

Masgelier, le 31/VII 42

_Ma chère maman! Je t'aime
beaucoup et je
voudrais que tu m'envoies des letres
et si tu voudrais venir passer tes
vacances je suis au château de Masgelier
je m'amuse bien ici.
Je t'envoie 2000 baisers._

Masgelier July 31, 1942

Dear Mama,

I love you so much and I would like
you to send me some letters and to
spend your holidays with me. I am at
the castle of Masgelier. I have a lot of
fun here. I send you 2000 kisses.

On that day, there were forty-four children present: fourteen were born in France, seven in Algeria, eight in Belgium, seven in Germany, seven in Austria, and one in Poland. There were nine children between four and seven years old, twenty between the ages of eight and ten, thirteen between eleven and thirteen, and two between the ages of sixteen and seventeen.

On April 13, 1944, thirty-four children were deported in convoy no. 71, two in convoy no. 73, two in no. 74, three in no. 75, and three in no. 76.

Of the forty-four children, seventeen saw both parents deported, twelve had their fathers deported, and ten more had their mothers deported.

Georgy was one of the privileged few whose parents had not been deported. Their situation allowed them to see Georgy from time to time, as Hauteville was not far from Izieu.

Georgy's parents, together with those of Charles Weltner, were the only ones to survive the war. Julius and Sérafine settled in Haifa, Israel. They never stopped searching for Georgy with the hope that he was still alive. They suffered every day of their lives, lives that ended almost at the same time for each of them: Julius died first on April 7, 1989, forty-five years to the day after Georgy was transferred from Lyon to Drancy. Sérafine followed Julius on November 1, 1989.

—Serge Klarsfeld

UGIF,2,rue du Petit St Jean,2
Montpellier.   Montpellier,le 20 Avril 43.

        Cher Monsieur,depuis 15 jours notre
maison de Lodève est liquidée et votre petit
Georgie se trouve actuellement dans les environs
de Montpellier dans très bonnes conditions et
en bonne santé.Il a été très content de retrouver
ici ses vieux amis de Chaumont,moi et ma fille,
et de povoir ainsi sortir de temps en temps de
sa pension.Nous le voyons tous les dimanches et
les jeudis.La semaine dernière nous l'avons ame-
né à la foire et il s'est beaucoup amusé.

UGIF, 2 rue du Petit St. Jean, 2
Montpellier, April 20, 1943

Dear Sir,
Fifteen days ago our home at Lodève was cleared out and
your little Georgy has been moved to a location near
Montpellier in good condition and in good health. He was
very happy to find his old friends from Chaumont here, my
daughter and me, as this enables him to leave his boarding
house from time to time. We see him every Sunday and
Thursday. Last week we took him to the fair and he had a
very good time.

Montpellier, le I4-V-43.

Cher Monsieur, j'ai reçu votre lettre ce matin-même et je m'empresse de vous répondre. Georgy quitte la région de Montpellier et s'en va dimanche, après-demain, dans le département de l'Ain. Voila sa future adresse : Maison d'enfants d'Yzieu par Bregnier-Cordon (AIN). Il sera là-bas avec le personnel de l'ancienne maison de Lodève, c.à d. dans les conditions que vous avez déjà pu apprécier et où les éducateurs le connaissent et l'aiment bien. Georgy a conservé son bon caractère qui le fait gâter par tout le monde et de cette façon il n'est jamais bien malheureux.

Ce le dernier de mes petits amis de Chaumont qui me quitte. Je le regrettrai d'autant plus qu'il se plaisait beaucoup à Montpellier où il est dans des conditions materielles, morales et de sécurité tout-à-fait exceptionnelles.

Dans l'Ain il ne sera, d'aileurs, qu'à quelques dizaines de kilomètres de sa maman et pourra certainement la voir souvent. J'ai écrit il y a à peine quelques jours à votre femme pour lui donner des nouvelles de Georgy. A ce moment rien n'était encore décidé définitivement au sujet du déplacement de Georgy et je vous serait bien obligé de prévenir par vos soins Madame Halpern et de lui faire savoir la nouvelle adresse de Georgy.

Montpellier, May 14, 1943

Dear Sir,

I received your letter this morning and haste to answer you. Georgy will leave the vicinity of Montpellier on Sunday, the day after tomorrow, for the department of Ain. Here is his address: Children's Home of Izieu near Bregnier-Cordon (Ain). There he will be with the staff of the old home of Lodève under conditions that you have already known to appreciate and where the educators know and like him. Georgy has kept his good character, which makes everyone want to spoil him, and as a result he is never very unhappy.

He is the last of my little friends from Chaumont to leave me. I will miss him especially. In Montpellier he was under exceptional material and moral security.

In Ain he will, among other things, only be some ten kilometers from his Mama and will certainly be able to see her frequently. Just a few days ago, I wrote to your wife to send her news about Georgy. At this moment nothing about Georgy's move has been definitely decided and I would appreciate your advising Mrs. Halpern of Georgy's new address.

il y a des grandes montagnes
et le village est très jolie il y
a beaucoup des fleurs et des arbres
et il y a beaucoup des fermes on
va des fois se promènai a
brenur-oraon la maison
est très belle on va cherche
des mûr noirs et blanche et
rouge je t'embrasse de
tout mon cœur.

There are big mountains and
the village is very beautiful. There
are many flowers and trees and
farms where we take walks. It is very
beautiful around the house. We are
going to pick black, white, and red
berries. I kiss you with all my heart.

Georgy

Cher papa.

J'ai bien reçu ton colis est la lettre qui m'a
fait un grand plaisir il y avai dans le colis
il y avai un cadecale des mouchoires des bonbons
des gâteaus du chocolat. Je m'excuse de ne pas
avair ecrie plus tôt je m'amuse bien avec mes
camarade. Je monge bien. pour noël J'ai reçu
une boite de piture est un cahier de dessin Je suis
en bonne santé il tombe pas encore de la neige
Je suis dans le cour élémentaire. es- tu en
bonne santé. quan setai noël on a fait une fête
on a jouer des pieses a gouter on a mangé
on a bu du borolmaltire un sac de bonbons
du pain- d'epice une gofrette de la pâte decoin
est du chocolat moi je me suis bien regaler
avec toutes ces friandises je vais à l'ecole
Je te souhaite une bonne est heureuse
année que la gerre finise bien tôt est l'on
sois touse reunie Je t'embrasse 1000000000
ton fils qui t'aime beaucoup.
GEORGY HALPERN.

Dear Papa,
I have received your package
and the letter which gave me
great pleasure. In the package
there were handkerchiefs,
sweets, cakes, and chocolates.
I excuse myself for not having
written to you sooner. I am
having a very good time with
my friends. For Christmas,
I received a box of paints and
a drawing book. I am well.
It has not snowed yet. I am in
elementary classes. Are you
well? At Christmas we produced
some plays; we ate different
things; we drank Ovaltine.
We received a bag of sweets,
gingerbread, a wafer, dried fruit,
paste, jam, and chocolate. I had
a real feast with all the treats.
I go to school and wish you a
good and happy new year. I kiss
you 1000000000 times. Your
son who loves you very much,

Georgy Halpern

17

Monday, October 31, 1943

Dear Mama,

Thank you very much for the package you sent me for my birthday. It gave me great pleasure. The card was very beautiful. I have the mittens, the modeling clay, the sugar, the biscuits, and the apples. Are you well? I am well. It is beginning to get cold here. We are beginning school. I am in the elementary classes. I go to church. Send me all my stamps even those I left at home. I kiss you with all my heart.

G. Halpern

lundi 31 octobre 1943.

chère maman.

Je te remerçi beaucoup du colis que tu ma envoye pour mon anniversaire. Il ma fait beaucoup plaisir. La cartre aite tres belle. J'ai bien reçu la paire de mouphe. est la pate a modelé. le decoupage est l'albome a coubaulorier le cucre les biscuis les pommes. es-tu en baome sente moi je va bien il comence a faire froit ici on fait l'ecole ici je suis dans le cours elémentére je vais a leglise envoye moi tout mes timbres méme selas que jojai levé a la maison je t'embrasse de tout mon cœur

G. HALPERN

Lundi 17 janvier 1944.

chère maman,

J'ai bien reçu ta carte qui m'a fait un grand plaisir, je me porte bien, je m'amuse bien, a noël on a fait des fête, on a jouer des pieces est on a bien manger, on a manger du pain d'épice, du chocolat chocolat, de la pâte de coin, un sac de bonbons, on a but du ovomaltine, est on a donné des jouets moi j'ai reçu une boite de pinture est un cahier de dessin, es-tu en bonne santé, la petite carte de bonne année était très belle, j'ai désir repondie a papa, il tombe pas encore de la neige je mange bien, je dor bien, je suis bien, on fait des promenades, le jeudi est le dimenche, on se leve à 7 eures, le matin on boit boivat du café une tartine avec de la confiture d-midi debai de la soupe potage un lecume du dêser a jouter du pain avec du chocolat du lait le soire une soupe un lecume du fromage blanc, je t'enrait mille 10 00 00 00 00 000 bese ton fils qui t'aime beaucoup

Dear Mama,

I have received your postcard which gave me great pleasure. I am well. I have fun. At Christmas we celebrated: we performed plays and had good food. We ate gingerbread, chocolate, dried fruit paste, a bag of sweets, and we drank Ovaltine. We received toys. I received a box of paints and a drawing book. Are you well? The little New Year card was beautiful. I already answered Papa. It still has not snowed. I eat well, I sleep well, I am well. We go on walks on Thursdays and on Sundays. We get up at 7 o'clock in the morning, we drink coffee and have a sandwich with jam, at noon sometimes a soup, vegetables, dessert, at snack-time bread with chocolate and milk, and at supper a soup, vegetables, and farmer cheese. I send you 1000000000 kisses. Your son who loves you very much.

chère maman
Je te remerci beaucoup de la lettre que tu ma envoyé, j'ai reçu le coli mais je ne né pas reçu les chaussure neuy Es-tu en bonne santé mais je me porte bien, je mamuse bien avec mes camarades, oui les chaussettes de tu ma envoye me vont très bien, ici il fait tr très beau, on ma rasser la tête mes mes cheuveus pousse vite je me brosse les dens tout les matins, avec le dentifrisse de que tu ma envoyé en classe je suis dans le cours élémentaire, j'ai un cahier, un buvar bleu, un porteplume, un crayon a mine et des crayons de couleurs, je mange bien, je dors bien, le cartable que tu ma envoyé il et très bien, je termine ma lettre en t'envoyent 1000000000000000000000000000000000000000000000000000000000000000000000000000000000000000000000000000000000000000000

Dear Mama,
Thank you for the letter you sent me. I received the package, but I did not receive the new shoes. Are you well? I am doing well. I have fun with my friends. Yes, the socks you sent me fit well. It is beautiful here.
They are going to shave my head; my hair grows fast.
I brush my teeth every morning with the toothpaste you sent me. In the elementary classes, I have a notebook, blue blotting paper, a pen, a pencil, and coloring pencils of my own.
I eat and sleep well. The school bag you sent me is very good.
I end my letter sending you
1OOOOOOOOOOOOOOOOOOOOOOOO
OOOOOOOOOOOOOOOOOOOOOOOO
OOOOOOOOOOOOOOOOOOOOOOOO
OOOOOOOOOOOOOOOOOOOOOOOO
OOOOOOOOOOOOOOOOOOOOOOOO
OOOOOOOOOOOOOOOOOOO kisses.

Friday, January 18, 1944

Dear Papa,

I received your package which gave me great pleasure. Thank you very much for the package; in the package there were cakes, a coloring book, and paints. I am well. We do compositions, I received fifty points; I am the fourth of six. It still has not snowed; it is still warm. I eat well. The classroom is pretty; it has two pictures, a stove, maps, drawings on the walls, and four windows. There are fifteen offices. I eat well. I send you 10000000000000 kisses. Your son who loves you very much.

Georgy

In the back there is a drawing. I would like you to send me toothpaste in a tube because I have none and an envelope with your address.

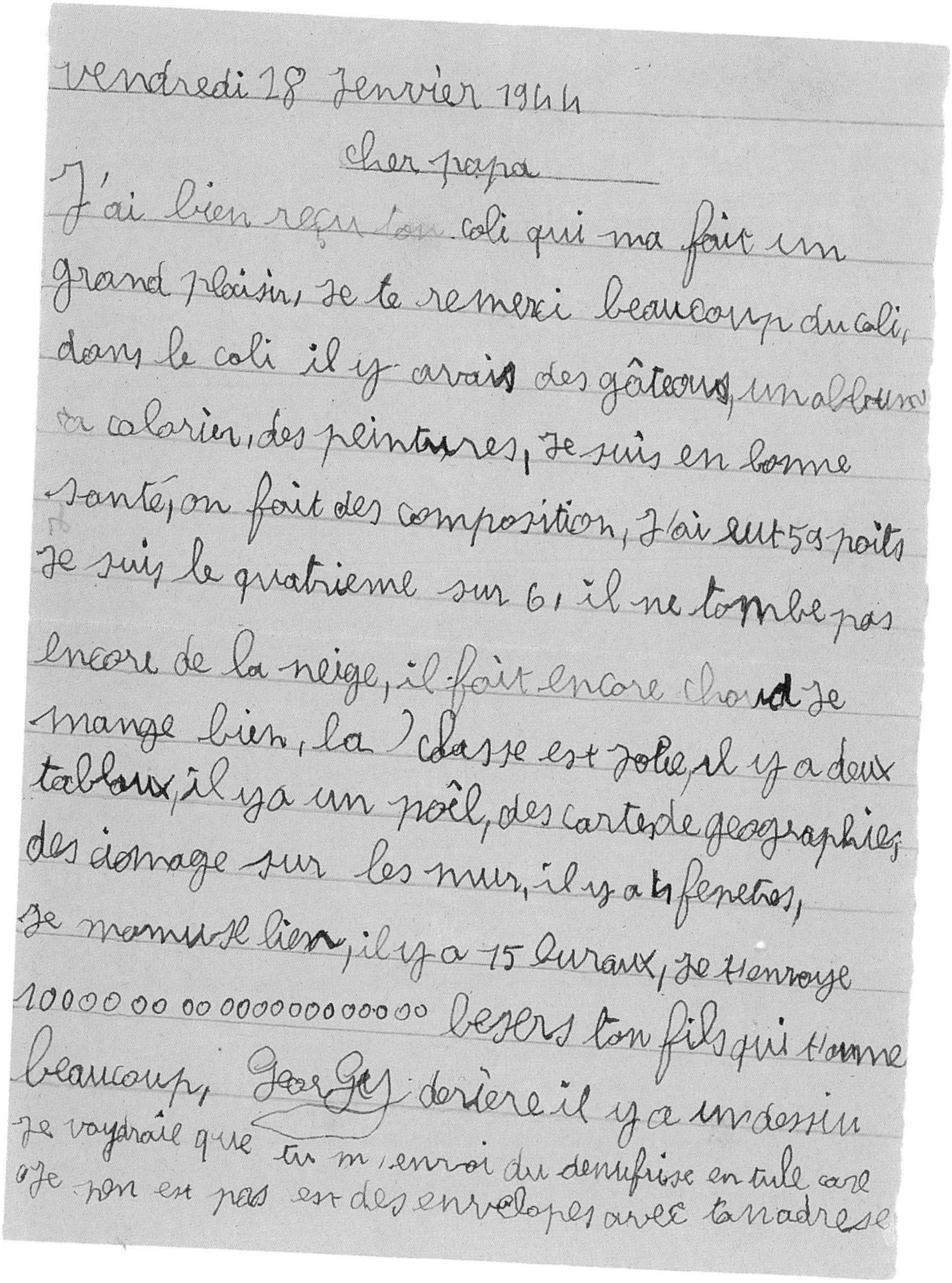

vendredi 18 Janvier 1944

cher papa

J'ai bien reçu ton coli qui ma fait un grand plaisir, je te remerci beaucoup du coli, dans le coli il y avais des gâteaux, un album a colorier, des peintures, Je suis en bonne santé, on fait des composition, J'ai eut 50 poits Je suis le quatrieme sur 6, il ne tombe pas encore de la neige, il fait encore chaud Je mange bien, la classe est jolie, il y a deux tablaux, il y a un poêl, des carte de geographie, des domage sur les mur, il y a 4 fenetres, Je mamuse bien, il y a 15 buraux, Je t'envoye 10000 00 00 0000000000000 besers ton fils qui t'aime beaucoup, Georgy deriere il y a un dessin Je voudrais que tu m'envoi du dentifrise en tule car Je n'en es pas es des envelopes avec ta adrese

24

samedi 9 fevrier 1944.

Chère maman,

j'ai bien reçu ta lettre est la photo qui
ma fait beaucoup plaisir. il tombe de la neige
mais il ne fait pas ecore très froid. il y a une
grande terasse ou c'on voit tout le paysage est
c'est très joli de voir toutes les montagne toute
couvertes de neige. il me menque des caleçontes des
caleçons et des chaussettes la directrise a
dit que tu menvoye 200 francs parce qu'elle a
un bon pour m'acheter des galoches. es-tu
en bonne santé? mai je me porte bien
je m'amuse bien a faire du travaux
je mange bien. je dors bien on se laive a
7 eures. je sui en bonne santé il y a
un chien qui s'apelle tomi. quand on marche
sur la neige la neige se cole a nous pieds.
mardi cra on va faire une fête. envoye
mais un bloc de papier a lettre ou qui li a
des très. et des evelopes avec ton adresse.
je t'envoye 10 00 000 00 00 0000 0 00000 00 00
ton fils qui t'aime beaucoup
Georgy

Dear Mama,

Thank you for your letter and the photo which gave me great pleasure. It is snowing but it is not very cold. There is a large terrace from where one can see the whole countryside and it is very beautiful to see all the mountains covered with snow. I need pants, underpants, and socks. The director says that you should send me 200 francs because she has a rationing coupon to buy me overshoes. Are you well? I am fine. I enjoy doing my work. I eat well. I sleep well. We get up at 7 o'clock. I am in good health. There is a dog whose name is Tomi. When we walk in the snow, the snow sticks to our feet. Tuesday we had a party. Send me a block of writing paper.

Georgy

lundi le 28 février 1944

chère maman

j'ai bien reçu ta lettre et ton colis qui m'a fait beaucoup ~~beau~~ beaucoup plaisir ~~et tu en bonne~~ je me porte bien. il y a de la neige il y a un garçon qui a une luge et il m'a la prêté est c'est très amusant de faire de la neige ~~sur la luge~~ parce que il y a une ~~tente~~ ~~je mange~~ bientôt il ne fait pas très froid il fait un peu chaud et c'est très ~~joli de voir~~ tout la campagne couvert de neige mais elle a vite fondu ~~parce que il pleut beaucoup~~ mardi gras on a fait une fête on avait cinq jours de vacances on m'a rasé la tête je te termine ma lettre en t'envoyllant 1000.000.000.000.000.000. 000.000.000.000.000.000.000.000.000.000.000. 000.000.000.000.000.000.000.000.000.000.000. BESERS. ton fils qui t'aime beaucoup et qui pense beaucoup a toi mille BESERS

Monday, February 28, 1944

Dear Mama,
I received your letter and your package which gave me great pleasure. Are you well? I am well. It snows here. There is a boy who has a sled and he lends it to us. It is lots of fun to go sledding because we have a hill. I eat well. It is not very cold, it is a little warm and very beautiful to see all the mountains covered with snow, but unfortunately the snow has disappeared quickly. On Ash Wednesday, we will have five days of vacation. I erased a lot of the beginning of this letter. I end by sending you 1000000000000000000 00000 00000000000000000 kisses. Your son who loves you very much and who thinks of you often.

Georgy

Friday, March 14, 1944

Dear Mama,

Thank you very much for the letter you sent me. Are you well? I am well and am having a good time with my friends from the colony. I know many songs and I do many recitations. I am in good health. I eat well and I sleep well. It is very nice here. There is a boy who has a football. He is nice and lends it to us. We have fun playing with it. In the morning, we have writing and math classes. In the afternoon, we do a dictation and grammar homework. Once we know the lesson, we recite verb conjugations and the multiplication table for 3, 4, 5, 6, 7, 8, and 9. We also write compositions. I received sixty-nine and a half points, and was the third of eight. I end this letter sending you 10000000000000000 kisses. Your son who loves you very much and who thinks of you often.

vendredi 24 mars 1944
Chère maman
Je te remerci beaucoup de la lettre que
tu ma envoyé ~~je~~ as-tu en bonne santé
moi je me porte bien, je mamuse bien
avec mes camarade de la colonie. Je sais
beaucoup de chansons et ~~je~~ Je sais beaucoup
de résitasions, je suis en bonne santé. Je
mange bien je dors bien. Il fait beau ici,
il y a un carçon qui a un balon de foutebale
alor on samuse avec se balon car il nous
le prêté car il est gentil. en classe le matin
on fait de l'ecriture du calcul. lapré midi
on fait une dictée ou un devoir de grammaire
et quand on sore on aprent des leçon.
une resilation des verbes la table de 1 de 2 de
3 de 4 de 5 de 6 de 7 de 8 de 9 ~~et~~ de dix. on
fait des compositions j'ai eu 64 points edemi
j'ai etait le 3 troisième sur 8 je termine
ma lettre en tembrasent 100,000.000.000.
000,000.000.000.000.000.000.000.000.000.000.000.
000.000.000.000.000.000.100 000 00000 00000000
ton fils qui t'aime bocoup est qui pence

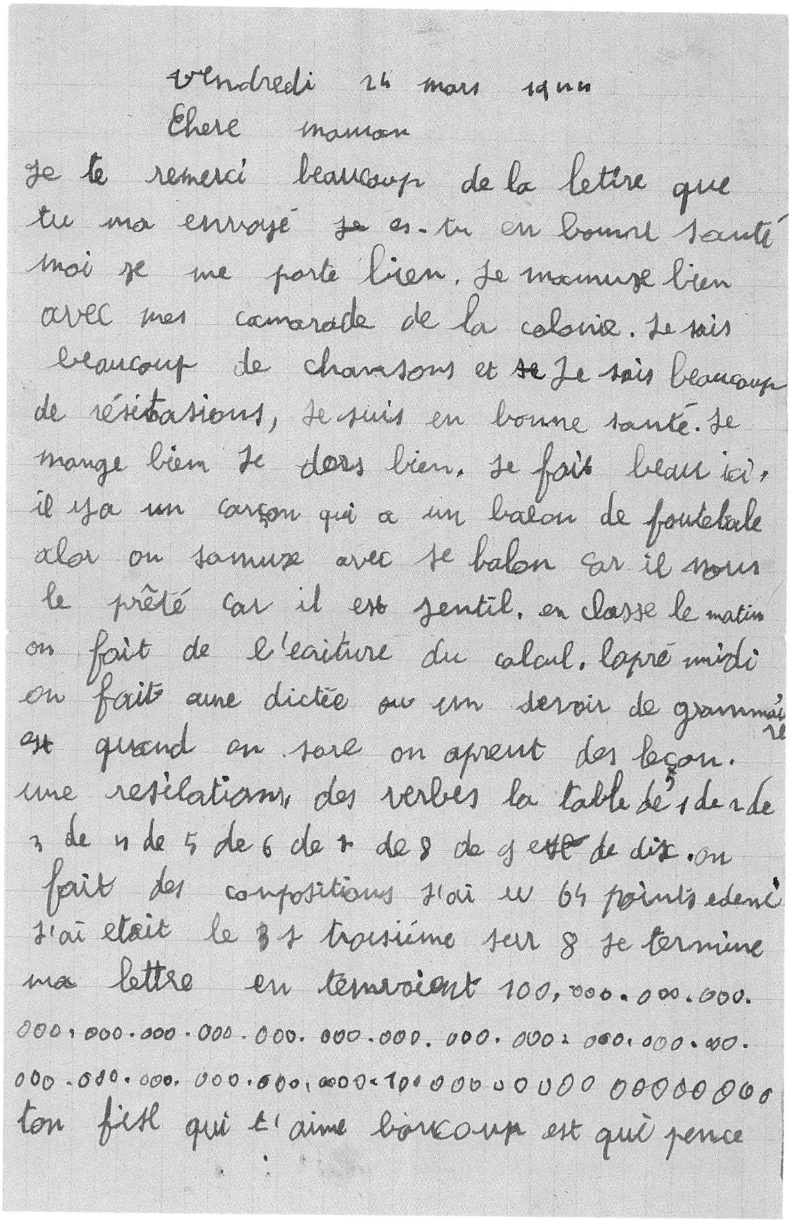

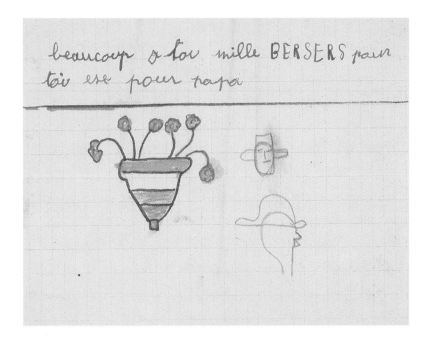

A thousand KISSES for you and for Papa.

Georgy with friends from the House of Izieu

vendredi 17 mars 1944

Cher papa :

J'ai te remercié beaucoup du coli et de la lettre qui m'a fait beaucoup plaisir dont dans le coli il y avais des gâteaux les bonbons du dentifrice en tube je m'amuse bien avec mes camarades ...

Je me porte bien en classe je suis le troisième sur 8 j'ai eu 64 points ...
fait des compositions d'écriture, de calcul, de ..., de grammaire de histoire de France de géographie de leçon de ... chose, je mange bien je dors bien on fait des promenades les jeudi et les dimanche quand il fait beau on m'a rasé la tête je termine ma lettre en t'envoient 1000.000.000.000,0...

ton fils qui pense beaucoup à toi et à papa mille baiser pour maman et pour papa !

POUR MAMAN

Friday, March 17, 1944

Dear Papa,

Thank you very much for your package and the letter; they gave me great pleasure. In the package there were cakes, sweets, and toothpaste in a tube. I am having a good time with friends here. Are you well? I am doing well in class. I am the third of eight. I received a point and a half for serious compositions, math, science, grammar, French history, and geography. I eat well; I sleep well; I go for walks on Thursdays and Saturdays if the weather is good. I had my head shaved. I end this letter by sending you 100000000000 kisses. Your son who thinks of you often. A thousand kisses for mama and papa!

Madame

Serafine Halpern

l'esperense Hauteville

(AIN) par fressier

Opposite: *Envelope addressed by Georgy to his mother dated March 6, 1944, sent from the post office in Bregnier-Cordon.*

Envelopes sent to Georgy from his mother on April 6, 1944, the day the House of Izieu was raided.

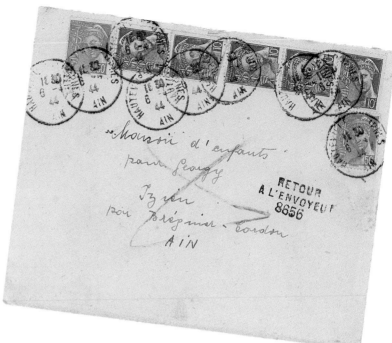

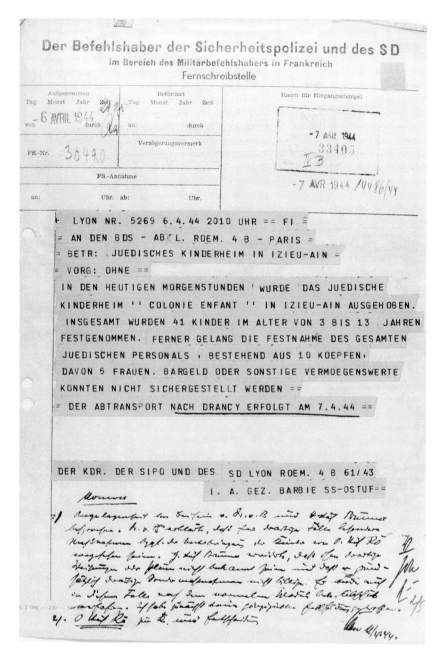

In den heutigen Morgenstunden wurde das Jüdische Kinderheim "Colonie Enfant" in Izieu-Ain ausgehoben. Insgesamt wurden 41 Kinder im Alter von 3 bis 13 Jahren festgenommen. Ferner gelang die Festnahme des gesamten Jüdischen Personals, bestehend aus 10 Köpfen, davon 5 Frauen. Bargeld oder sonstige Vermögenswerte konnten nicht sichergestellt werden.

Announcement in German of the security police S.D. in the jurisdiction of the military region of France e34tc... The translation reads:

> Lyon No. 5269, April 6, 1944 at 20 h.10
> At BDS section Roem 4B Paris
> Subject: The Jewish Children's Home at Izieu (Ain). Early this morning, the Jewish children's home, "children's Colony" at Izieu (Ain) was raided. A total of forty-one children aged three to thirteen years were captured, as well as the entire Jewish staff consisting of ten individuals, including five women. Cash or other valuables could not be secured. The transport to Drancy will take place on July 4, 1944.
>
> The Commandant of the Sipo and the S.D. at Lyon. Roem 4B 61/43
> Per order
> Signed: BARBIE,
> S.S. Obersturmführer

It should be noted that there were forty-four children: but because of their age and also probably their maturity, Arnold Hisch (seventeen), Théodor Reis (sixteen), and Fritz Loebmann were considered staff, and were included with the adults (ten), reducing the number of children (forty-one).

1. The manual annotations to the manuscript were added in Paris at the Service of Jewish Affairs.

A major piece of evidence at the trial of Barbie: a telex by which the chief of the Gestapo of Lyon announced the liquidation of the House of Izieu. The original document was uncovered by Serge Klarsfeld, among a file deposited in the cellar of the Center of Contemporary Jewish Documentation.

The daily arrivals booklet in Drancy records the arrival of the children of Izieu on April 8, 1944, with their names and sometimes false identities.

OSE

OEUVRE DE SECOURS AUX ENFANTS

DIRECTION CENTRALE : 62, RUE SPONTINI

Téléphone :
PASSY 99-88

PARIS (XVI°)

Adresse Télégraphique.
OSENFANTS - PARIS

LE 18 AVRIL 194 5

SERVICE
DU REGROUPEMENT FAMILIAL

LL.

Monsieur Jules H A L P E R N

NEUVIC D'USSEL.

MINISTÈRE
DES
ANCIENS COMBATTANTS
ET
VICTIMES DE GUERRE

Direction de l'Etat Civil &
des Recherches

Missions et Recherches
5° Bureau

83, Avenue/Foch Paris 16°
abd 5 n° R.
hm.yb.   13811

CENTRAL COMMITTEE OF JEWS IN POLAND
WARSAW, Sienna Str. 60

370/e4

Varsovie, le 19-ième Février 1948

RADA ŽIDOVSKÝCH NÁBOŽENSKÝCH OBCÍ V ZEMÍCH ČESKÉ A MORAVSKOSLEZSK
PRAHA V, MAISLOVA 18.

CENTRAL COMMITTEE OF LIBERATED JEWS
IN THE AMERICAN OCCUPIED ZONE IN GERMANY

V Praze dne 6.I.1948.

UNITED KINGDOM SEARCH BUREAU FOR GERMAN AUSTRIAN AND STATELESS PERSONS FROM CENTRAL EUROPE.

Telephone : MUSeum 6811

BLOOMSBURY HOUSE
BLOOMSBURY STREET
LONDON,   W.C.I

AMERICAN RED CROSS
NATIONAL HEADQUARTERS
WASHINGTON 13, D.C.
January 2, 1947

Nous sommes désolées de vous faire savoir que toutes les recherches concernant votre enfant que nous avons faite à la suite
de votre lettre du 25 Avril sont restées sans succès.

Julius and Sérafine Halpern never stopped their search for Georgy.
Whenever it was possible they wrote to everyone they could, as demonstrated
by the clippings above and on the opposite page.

COMITÉ INTERNATIONAL DE LA CROIX-ROUGE

AGENCE CENTRALE DES PRISONNIERS DE GUERRE

Rappeler dans la réponse :

Service Français
DF 8o7.21

Chèques postaux 1. 5527
Téléphone 4 23 05
Télég. "INTERCROIXROUGE"   PJ/pyt

GENÈVE, 5 Décembre 1947

CENTRAL TRACING BUREAU.
P.C.I.R.O.
APO. 171.   400. BAOR.

Date. 20th August, 1947.

RAEL. KULTUSGEMEINDE WIEN

in Ihrem Antwortschreiben
nachstehendes Zeichen anzuführen

3/LW/956o/1734

Madame Sérafine HALPERN
118, Rue Charonne

Cher Monsieur,

Nous avons bien reçu votre lettre du II crt. et nous avons le regret de vous informer que votre enfant ne figure malheureusement pas sur la liste des déportés libérés et actuellement en SUISSE.

DEUTSCHES ✚ ROTES KREUZ

SUCHDIENST HAMBURG

FÉDÉRATION DES SOCIÉTÉS JUIVES DE FRANCE

SERVICE DE RECHERCHES DES DÉPORTÉS ET REGROUPEMENT DES FAMILLES

9, Rue Guy-Patin, PARIS (10ᵉ)

Central Jewish Committee
Bergen-Belsen
Mil. Gov. 618 B.A.O.R.
Telefon: 671, 351, 376

In Beantwortung Ihres Schreibens vom 14. 11.d.J. müssen wir Ihnen zu unserem grössten Bedauern mitteilen, dass wir über Herrn Georg Halpern nichts feststellen konnten.

194 6   7 Mai

My dear Madame Halpern:

MINISTÈRE DES PRISONNIERS DE GUERRE, DÉPORTÉS ET RÉFUGIÉS

With reference to your letter of December 8th, concerning your son, George, We are indeed sorry that we have no way of obtaining information about him for you.

Nous avons le regret de vous informer que le nom de M. HALPERN Georges ne figure pas à ce jour sur les Listes des Libérés que nous possédons.

Schweizer Hilfswerk für Emigrantenkinder

Comité suisse d'aide aux enfants d'émigrés

ZENTRALSTELLE: Claridenstrasse 36, Telephon 270800

As late as 1982, Julius and Sérafine Halpern had not stopped looking for their child and even on the very night preceding Barbie's return to France they were still publishing personal advertisements in the Israeli press.

Letter from Sérafine Halpern to Beate Klarsfeld (February 1986):

"I often think of you and have been wanting to write to you for some time now. How I would have loved to talk to you but as you must have noticed yourself, it was impossible. Each time the subject is George, I feel my heart break and cannot speak a word. Unfortunately, my memory is very good and I am tormented day and night by the visual images of the daily events during the time that Georgy was with us. I cannot forget anything. He was such a charming boy, so lively, intelligent, and full of joy. I once met a woman who, after having lost her son in an accident, lost her memory. How lucky she was! We try to live a normal life; we go out and meet other people. But wherever we are, the same question is asked: "Have you any children?" We answer "no," but the whole evening is ruined because it causes my absolute unhappiness to resurface. Such is life. Nobody suspects a thing, as I put on a strong façade."

Halpern Julius and Sera Fine request information and details on their son

George Halpern

born October 30, 1935 and taken away by the Germans on April, 1944 from Izieux, France to Auschwitz.

Anyone with information on the above is requested to contact the Halpern family, 27 Rehov Shimkin, Haifa, **Tel. 04-246056.**

AVIS DE RECHERCHE

Julius et Seraphine Halpern, demandent des informations à tous ceux qui ont connu leur fils, Georges Halpern, né le 30 octobre 1935, raflé par les Allemands en avril 1944 à Iziev en France et déporté à Auschwitz.

Prière de téléphoner à la famille Halpern, 27 rue Shimkin - Haifa - Tel : 04 - 24 60 56.

COURS DES CHANGES
AU 26 MAI 1982

Julius, Sérafine, and Georgy Halpern, 1942

Julius and Sérafine Halpern, 1969

THE UNDER-PREFECT OF BELLEY

Belley, April 3, 1946

Sir,

So that the memory of the martyrs
of Izieu remain forever engraved in our
minds, their friends took the initiative
to install a plaque on the house and erect a
monument at the intersection of the roads
Belley-Izieu-Bregnier-Cordon.

Two ministers, as well as the Ambassador of
Canada, and the Reverend Father Chaillet
will be present to officiate at the unveiling,
which will take place next April 7th at 3 P.M.

I understand that it will be painful for you
to relive the tragedy, which hit you so cruelly
in your most beloved affections but I think
that you will want to know the place where
your child lived happily and witness the
public honor to be bestowed on all those
little ones.

LE SOUS-PRÉFET
DE
BELLEY

BELLEY, LE ___3 avril 1946___ 194

Monsieur,

Pour que le souvenir des
martyrs d'IZIEU reste à jamais
gravé dans les esprits, leurs
amis ont pris l'initiative d'appo-
ser une plaque sur la maison et
d'ériger une stèle au carrefour
des routes BELLEY - IZIEU -
BREGNIER-CORDON.

Deux ministres, ainsi que
Monsieur l'Ambassadeur du CANADA
et le Révérend Père CHAILLET
ont été pressentis pour présider
cette inauguration qui se déroulera
le 7 avril prochain à 15 Hres.

Je comprends qu'il vous soit
douloureux de vivre la tragédie
qui vous a si cruellement frappé
dans vos affections les plus chères
mais je pense que vous aimerez
connaître les lieux où votre
enfant vécu heureux et être témoin
de l'hommage public rendu à la
mémoire de tous ces petits.

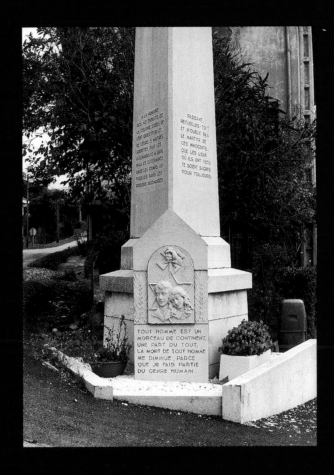

*Monument dedicated to the children of Izieu on April 6th, 1987, the National
Day of Commemoration of the Deportation, in the city of Nantua Cain.*

SERGE KLARSFELD'S PLEA ON BEHALF OF THE CHILDREN OF IZIEU, JUNE 17, 1987, LYON

Mr. President, Councilors, Ladies and Gentlemen of the Jury. The trial of Klaus Barbie is an historic trial: he is the first person in France to be tried on the grounds of crimes against humanity. The accused is to be judged in accordance with the law of December 26, 1964, unanimously voted in by Parliament and aimed at crimes committed by the Nazis and by their accomplices.

We are dealing here with the first trial; we may be dealing with only one if we do not obtain a verdict for the two highly placed officials of the police and the administration of Vichy, against whom we have also brought action for crimes against humanity. I am speaking of Jean Leguay and Maurice Papon.

It is certainly not necessary to emphasize to you, who have attended the twenty-four, often moving, hearings of this trial, the importance conferred on this trial both here in France and around the world. The trial of Klaus Barbie is the final episode in this vast criminal case resulting from the operations undertaken nearly forty-five years ago by the Gestapo of Lyon under the leadership of Klaus Barbie.

It should be noted that the following events succeeded each other: the merciless hunt for Jewish families to send them to extermination camps, as well as the cruel repression of resistance workers through torture, deportation, and collective executions; Barbie's use of the American special services while they held an occupied zone in Germany; the protection they granted Barbie when faced with the many requests by the French government to have him handed over to the French courts; Barbie's escape to South America arranged for him by these same special services; the contradictory trial of a few officials of the Lyon Gestapo and the in absentia death sentences Barbie received in 1952 and 1954; the dismissal of the case decided upon by the Prosecution in Munich in 1971 in favor of the phantom criminal that Barbie had become and its revocation a few months later due to new testimonies; the discovery of Barbie that same year (1971); the shock on his face and his lies—"I am not Barbie"—on our television screens; the refusal of the Bolivian dictators to have him extradited; Barbie's triumphant ten-year long impunity; the thunderclap of his forced return to France, to the very places of his crimes in spite of the time that had passed and the distance he had put between himself and France; finally, his provocative defense that intended to transform himself, the former chief of the Lyon Gestapo, from the accused into the accuser.

Legally this trial could very well not have taken place. The limitation of action by lapse of time was played out in Barbie's favor: twenty years after his two in absentia death sentences, coupled with the authority of the item judged.

Thus, Barbie is not being judged for all of his crimes. He is being charged neither for those perpetrated in the Saint-Claude region, nor for the atrocious executions he ordered in Bron and in Saint-Genis-Laval. If, in 1964, Barbie's military judges had been perfectionists not one item of business would have remained unknown, not one item of business would have been forgotten. Everything would have been judged; everything would have been specified.

In addition, had the Gestapo been a criminal organization that was absolutely meticulous even in their collapse, there would not have been a single escapee from the prisons and camps; not a single one of these witnesses who have testified here with such dignity would have been left alive; not a single one of the documents would have been spared from the fire, such as the telex of Izieu that I was able to find. For without eyewitnesses and documentary evidence, Barbie could not have been tried.

The fact of having put an end to Barbie's interminable flight, the fact of being able to bring action against him legally even if only for part of his crimes, are two opportunities that allow us to bring an end to a legal action, which is linked to an action of memory. It is through remembrance but also through taking action, that the executioner of the children of Izieu will be prevented from knowing an untroubled old age enlivened by the complacent account of his Hitlerian exploits. For as a young S.S. lieutenant, he used to reign over Lyon through police violence with more power over life and death in his hands than a general of the Wehrmacht had.

During the twenty-one months he spent in Lyon, as the leader of Section IV of the Sipo-S.D., as head of the Gestapo, Barbie came to be known, and will always be known as "the butcher of Lyon." As we have heard here over and over again, this middle-ranking official of Nazi terror did not confine himself to defending the security of the occupying forces, but instead unleashed himself against his victims with the sadism of physical and moral torture. His fanaticism, too, led him to take the initiative and the personal and complete responsibility for homicidal operations of enormous proportions, such as the roundups of Izieu and the Rue Sainte-Catherine, the final deportation of August 11, 1944, and a few days later, the massacre of those he could no longer deport to Auschwitz or Dachau, whom he preferred to assassinate rather than accept the prospect of their imminent liberation by the Allies.

Throughout his criminal activities, did Barbie retain his free will and a clear awareness of good and evil? I sincerely believe he did. He had received a sound education and was from an honorable family; in his racial file from 1940 he states that he "believes in God;" but he did choose to join the S.S. and to make his career in the S.D. He who apparently began to read Homer again knew that, like Hercules, he had a choice between the path of good and the path of evil.

He made his choice and later, as the head of the Gestapo of Lyon, he willingly entered the realm of cruelty and horror beyond what the Führer, his leader, or his superiors—Knorhen, Oberg, Lischka, Hagen or Knab—demanded from him directly.

When Barbie annihilated the home of the children of Izieu, neither the Berlin nor the Paris S.S. had requested that of him. In that year, 1944, only Alois Brunner was to follow Barbie's example and on July 20th, subsequently destroyed the homes of Jewish children in the Paris region.

That is why, both in Damascus and in La Paz, Beate and I went to campaign in opposition to Brunner and Barbie's impunity. We did so in the memory of those children of Izieu whose lives Barbie terminated one spring day in 1944 with the roundup that was to lead them to the precipice of Birkenau-Auschwitz, where, in 1943, I myself at the age of eight would have gone with my father had not the fragile double wall of a closet saved me from the searches of Brunner and his Gestapo men.

No, Jacques Vergès, this was not a search, it was a roundup and from the other side of the wall I could hear the S.S. beating our neighbors' little girls, just as Barbie beat Simone Kadosche, in order to get them to disclose their older brother's address.

This was happening in Nice in September 1943. It was the Germans, the Germans alone who were responsible, in both Nice and Izieu. Since September 1942, the Vichy police had been cooperating less and less with the persecution of Jews, which it had been involved with on a massive scale during the summer of 1942 under the initiative of Oberg, the superior chief of the S.S. and of the German police in France. The persecution had been given the green light by the head of the government, Laval, and the head of state, Pétain. It had not only been done in the occupied zone—everyone remembers the roundup in the winter velodrome—but it had been carried out in the free zone as well, from where they had delivered 10,000 stateless or foreign Jews, who were then transferred to the transit camp of Drancy in the occupied zone to be deported to the East. Among them were the parents of most of the children of Izieu.

However, this massive cooperation was suddenly interrupted in the wake of the great roundup of the free zone on August 26, 1942, which had aroused the indignation of the French population, following the example of its spiritual guides, the highly placed Catholic and Protestant clergy whose public and thoughtful speeches caused Vichy great consternation. Troubled by this unexpected resistance from the public, Laval informed Oberg and Knochen and obtained their agreement that henceforth he would no longer be expected to deliver contingents of Jews.

That is how the Gestapo, which had been sending three trainloads of a thousand Jews each to Auschwitz on a weekly basis for eleven weeks, had to forgo its deportation program planned from September 15 to October 31, 1942: forty-five days, forty-five trains; the sudden burst of conscience of the French people had just saved the lives of 45,000 Jews. More than any other factor, this general compassion of the French, leaving aside a small minority of informers, militia members or Gestapo henchmen, explains the exceptional outcome of the "Final Solution" in France as compared to almost all other occupied European countries—with the exception of Denmark—where 80,000 Jews had perished and 240,000 survived.

French Jews will always remember that although the Vichy regime ended in moral bankruptcy, and was dishonored by contributing to the loss of a quarter of the Jewish population of the country, the remaining three quarters basically owe their survival to the sympathy of the French, as well as to their active solidarity from the moment they understood that Jewish families who had been seized by the Gestapo were doomed to die.

In April 1944, four or five months before the Liberation, the Gestapo in the provinces was the only group still turning innumerable victims over to Drancy to feed the trains of death. The numbers these hunters yielded would vary according to the K.D.S. The one in Lyon, where Barbie controlled the Jewish section, turned out to be the most efficient of all. He was the first Nazi officer to attack a home of Jewish children without hesitation.

Before my friend, Charles Libman, addresses the file on Barbie's responsibility in the Izieu affair, I would like to invoke the memory of each one of these children, whose civil state and sorrowful personal journey I have set out to reconstruct after having registered them in "The Memorial of the Deportation of French Jews," so that the executioner or falsifiers of history will not be able to claim, as has ludicrously been the case for the Izieu telex, that this did not involve real children or real victims.

SAM ADELSHEIMER was only five years old. He was born in Mannheim. His mother, Laura, had been deported on November 20, 1943, nine convoys before his. Sam did not return.

MAX LEINER was also born in Mannheim. He was seven. Max did not return.

The parents of OTTO WERTHEIMER were deported on August 17, 1942, transferred by Vichy from the free zone to Drancy in the occupied zone. He stayed behind alone; he was twelve years old. He was deported under the false identity of Octave Wermet. Otto did not return.

EGON GAMIEL was eight years old. His parents, Ernst and Gertrud, who both interned at the camp of Milles, which was handed over to the S.S. by Vichy, were deported on August 17, 1942. Egon did not return.

ARNOLD HIRSCH was Egon Gamiel's cousin. He had just turned seventeen and was the oldest of the forty-four children. His parents, Max and Ida, were in the same camp, the same convoy, and suffered the same fate as that of his cousin. Arnold himself was not gassed in Auschwitz: he was deported in the convoy of May 15, 1944 with Mr. Zlatin, and was shot in Estonia in the fortress of Reval. Arnold did not return.

THEO REISS was sixteen years old. Incarcerated in the camp of Gurs with his mother and grandmother, he lost them when Vichy handed them over to the Gestapo; they were deported on August 14, 1942. The memory of this cheerful adolescent was evoked right here by his friend Paul Niedermann. Theo did not return: he, too, was summarily executed in the fortress of Reval.

François Loban's real name was FRITZ LOBMANN. He was born in Mannheim; he was fifteen; his mother Mathilde was handed over to the S.S. and deported on August 17, 1942. François (Fritz) did not return. Together with Arnold and Theo he was one of the three adolescents taken for adults by Barbie in the abject accounts of his telex: forty-one children from three to thirteen and ten heads: ten heads as if it had to do with cattle; in reality, then, forty-four children and seven adults.

HANS AMENT was born in Vienna. He was ten years old. In Izieu they called him Jeannot. His father was deported on March 4, 1943. Not far from Izieu his mother was dying of tuberculosis; this is what he wrote to her:

> *"When there was a lot of snow here, we went sledding on the slopes. We had a really good time. Tell Freddy not to write to me in German. At the children's home there's a beautiful dog named Tomi. The school is in the house. There is a special teacher to run the school. She is a good teacher."*

Jeannot did not return.

The parents of GEORGY HALPERN survived only to weep daily over the loss of their only child. They did not have the strength to come here and evoke the memory of this eight year old boy, born in Vienna, who had written them so many touching letters from Izieu:

> *"Dear Mama,*
> *I got your postcard which gave me great pleasure. I am well. I have fun. At Christmas we celebrated: we performed plays and had good food. We ate gingerbread, chocolate, dried fruit paste, a bag of sweets, and we drank Ovaltine. We received toys. I received a box of paints and a drawing book. Are you well? The little New Year's card was beautiful. I already*

Egon Gamiel

Otto Wertheimer and
Fritz Lobmann

Hans Ament

Max Leiner

Arnold Hirsch

answered Papa. It still has not snowed. I eat well, I sleep well, I am well. We go on walks on Thursdays and on Sundays. We get up at 7 o'clock in the morning; we drink coffee, have toast and jam, at noon we sometimes a soup, vegetables, dessert; at snacktime bread with chocolate and milk; and at supper a soup, vegetables, and farmer's cheese. I send you 1000000000000 kisses. Your son who loves you very much.

There are big mountains and the village is very beautiful. There are many flowers and trees and farms where we take walks. It is very beautiful around the house. We are going to pick black, white, and red berries. I kiss you with all my heart."

Georgy did not return.

RENATE and LIANE KROCHMAL were also born in Vienna; they were eight and six years old. Their parents, Jacob and Amalie, were handed over to the Nazis by Vichy and were deported on September 16, 1942. As for their brother, Siegfried, he died in the camp of Rivesaltes at the age of eleven. Renate and Liane did not return.

MARTHA and SENTA SPIEGEL were ten and nine years old. They were born in Vienna. Rachel, their mother, and Aron, their father, were also handed over to the S.S. by Vichy and deported on September 25, 1942. Neither Martha nor Senta returned.

SIEGMUND SPRINGER was born in Vienna. He was eight years old. His parents, Mendel and Sarah, made the ominous trip organized by Vichy from the free zone to Drancy and were deported on September 11, 1942. Siegmund did not return.

Having recently arrived in Izieu, NINA ARONOW-ICZ wrote to her aunt:

"I'm very happy to be here; there are beautiful mountains and from the top of the mountains you can see the Rhône River passing by and that's very beautiful. Yesterday we went swimming in the Rhône with Miss Marcelle (she is a teacher). On Sunday we had a little party in honor of

Paulette's birthday and two other little ones and we put on a lot of plays and it was really great. And on July 25th we're having another party in honor of the children's home."

Nina was eleven; she was born in Brussels. Her mother, Mieckla, was deported on September 11, 1942 in the summer; her father, Leib, on December 7, 1943 in the fall, and she on April 13, 1944 in the spring. Nina did not return.

ALBERT BULKA, the youngest victim of Izieu, was born in Antwerp; MAJER-MARCEL BULKA, the oldest, was born in Poland. On the morning of the roundup, he was coming back from the middle school of Belley. In 1946, the principal of the school wrote:

"I see you before me, Marcel Bulka, a hardworking and proud boy, willing, delicate and discreet at the same time; prematurely grown up through anguish, so marvelously aware of his duties as the oldest one, having become head of the family at age thirteen. I see your little brother, Coco, again, a blond child of four, escaped from the camp of Agde underneath Madame Zlatin's coat; his eyes would light up with brotherly trust when you would hold his hand."

Their mother, Roizel had been deported on September 11, 1942 and their father, Mosiek, on March 4, 1943. Neither Marcel nor Coco returned.

In this very place, you have seen the father of LUCIENNE FRIEDLER speak of the loss in Izieu of his wife Mina and of his little girl of five. Isidore Friedler came back from Auschwitz; neither Mina nor Lucienne returned. He does not even have a photograph left of his daughter.

As for Max Mermelstein, his critical state of health did not to allow him to come from Australia to speak to you about his children, PAULA, ten years old, and seven year old MARCEL, both born in Antwerp, and about his wife, Frieda, who together with his children was arrested following the roundup of Izieu, on May 20th. Neither Paula, Marcel, nor their mother returned.

MAX and HERMANN TETELBAUM were also born in Antwerp. They were twelve and ten. Their arrest in Izieu led to that of their mother, Sefa, their sister Gabrielle, and their brother Maurice, caught a few days later in Chambéry. Of this family of six, unfortunately only the father survived.

Léa Feldblum, the only one to survive the roundup, suffered so much that she cannot coherently express everything she saw and endured. That admirable woman, Léa Feldblum, who chose to be deported immediately in order not to abandon the children who were in her charge, was holding Coco Bulka by one hand and ÉMILE ZUCKERBERG by the other when they came off the train in Birkenau. Émile was only five years old; he was born in Antwerp; his parents, Ziegmund and Serla, had been handed over to the Gestapo by Vichy and deported on September 14, 1942. For hours on end, she had to tell stories to this little boy, traumatized by the brutal separation, so that he would fall asleep; it was he who used to say: "When I'm big, I'm going to kill all the Krauts." Émile did not get to be big; he did not return from Auschwitz.

ESTHER, ELIE, and JACOB BENASSAYAG were born in Oran; they were twelve, ten, and eight. Their father had been arrested in the great roundup of Marseille and was deported on March 23, 1943. Esther, Elie, and Jacob did not return; but their mother still believes she sees them in the faces of those who are the same age as her children and who were lucky enough to become adults.

Fortunée Benguigui has been here to speak of her three children, JACQUES, RICHARD, and JEAN-CLAUDE, all three were also born in Oran. They were twelve, seven and five. Jacques is the one who on Mother's Day shared his packages with those friends of his who no longer had any parents. Fortunée, the unfortunate one, did come back from Auschwitz, but Jacques and Jean-Claude did not return.

BAROUK-RAOUL BENTITOU was always laughing and singing; he was twelve and was also born in the Oran region, in Palikao. His father and two of his brothers had already been deported on March 23, 1943. Barouk followed them and did not return either.

MAX and JEAN-PAUL BALSAM were born in Paris; they were twelve and ten years old. Their father had been deported with the first convoy of French Jews on March 27, 1942. Arrested in Paris with their grandmother in February 1943, they had been liberated from Drancy thanks to the U.G.I.F. that had helped them go to the southern zone while their grandmother was deported. In Izieu, Max and Jean-Paul enjoyed but a short respite. They did not return from Auschwitz.

CHAIM-HENRI and JOSEPH GOLDBERG were thirteen and twelve years old. They were born in Paris. Joseph sent drawings to his mother with the following letter:

"You tell me that I am a great artist as far as drawings go but I am no painter yet: only time will tell. As soon as we received your letter, we took it to the supervisor who read it to us and afterwards gave us a lesson in morality that I enjoyed listening to. She told us that we must study, otherwise when you see us again after the war, we'll just be dimwits. So I shall study well to make you happy, to make her happy, as well as the principal and my teacher, and to make me happy, too. That way after the war you'll see us both and we'll be intelligent not dimwits."

As for Henri, this is what the principal of the middle school of Belley said of him: "I see you before me. Henri Goldberg, little Parisian in love with life, with the fields, who became an enthusiastic farmer, but who remained spontaneous, rebellious and incredibly sassy and yet so sweetly helpful." Neither Henri nor Joseph returned.

You have seen and heard the testimony of Alexandre Halaunbrenner and his mother, Ita-Rosa. The two little girls, MINA and CLAUDINE, eight and five, were caught by Barbie's Gestapo. Their father, Jakob, and the oldest son, Leon, fourteen years old, were seized a few months later. The former was shot and the latter deported to Auschwitz from where he did not return. Mina and Claudine also did not return.

ISIDORE KARGEMAN was born in Paris; he was ten. His father had preceded him on June 5, 1942 in a convoy going to Auschwitz, from which Isidore did not return.

The Krochmal children

Majer and Albert Bulka

Martha and Senta Spiegel

Paula and Marcel Mermelstein

Nina Aronowicz

The Tetelbaum family

Theo Reiss

Unknown and Sarah Szulklaper

Max and Jean-Paul Balsam

Émile Zuckerberg

Raoul Bentitou

Jacques, Richard and Jean-Claude Benguigui

CLAUDE LEVAN-REIFMAN was the nephew of Dr. Reifman, who escaped the roundup and who has testified in this courtroom. Claude was ten years old; he was born in Paris; he was deported with his mother and his grandparents. Not one of them returned.

ALICE-JACQUELINE LUZGART was ten years old; she was born in Paris. Five days before the roundup she wrote to her sister:

> *"My dear sister,*
> *I received your letter dated March 28th, which made me very happy. Did you receive my letter in which I asked you for some sticks of rock candy and a few boxes of breath mints? I hope you got it and will do everything you can to send it to me as well as: stationery, envelopes, and ten stamps. Today is the first of April, you know, and also April Fool's Day, when they play tricks on you, this morning they played two tricks on me but I noticed it right away. I decided that I want to become an accountant but you know my classmate chose a nicer profession than I. When she is older she wants to become an intern in the maternity clinic as a student midwife. She told me that she would like to operate on mothers to help little children come into the world because she loves little babies. Don't you think that's a nice profession? Perhaps I'll change my mind and do what she's going to do."*

Alice did not return.

GILLES SADOWSKI was eight years old; he was born in Paris. His mother, Ruchla, had been deported on July 27, 1942; his father, Symcha, did not escape deportation either. Gilles did not return.

CHARLES WELTNER was nine years old; he was born in Paris. His mother, Marguerite, was Hungarian. When she came back from deportation she did not find her son again and has never given up hope that he is still alive.

SARAH SZULKLAPER was born in Paris. In Izieu they called her Suzanne. Her parents, Tauba and Huna, had been deported on July 18, 1943. She celebrated her eleventh birthday on February 5, 1944 and on that day her girlfriends in Izieu all wished her what they themselves also hoped for:

Mina Aronovicz: *"I wish you a very happy birthday; may you celebrate it with your parents next year. Our presents are very small but our wishes are very big."*

Senta Spiegel: *"I wish you a very happy birthday and may you find your parents again."*

Esther Benassayag: *"I am writing this note to you to make you happy on your birthday; may you find your parents again and may the war be over soon."*

Alice Luzgart: *"Today we wish you the best for your eleventh birthday; I hope that you'll be with your parents next year and the ones after that and also that you'll soon be back with them. I'm closing with many kisses. Your friend who will never forget you."*

Liliane Gerenstein: *"Unfortunately today is a day that is not like other birthdays. I'm closing this note with the wish that you'll be back with your parents on your next one."*

Just as her girlfriends, Sarah only joined her parents again in the smoke of the Auschwitz crematoria.

MAURICE GERENSTEIN was born in Paris; he was thirteen years old. He attended the middle school of Belley. His principal had stated:

"I see you still, Maurice Gerenstein, a virtuoso at thirteen, sensitive and secretive, at whose talent as pianist and composer your teachers and your classmates marveled, and whose sad and refined improvisations held sure promises of genius."

Maurice did not return; neither did his ten-year-old sister Liliane, born in Nice. Their parents, Chendla and Chapse, were deported on November 20, 1943. It was LILIANE, age ten, who wrote this heartbreaking letter to God, which was found in Izieu:

"God? You are so good, you are so kind, and if we had to count the number of good and kind things you have done for us it would never end.... God? You are in charge. You are justice, you reward the good and punish the bad. God? I will never forget you. I will always think of you, even in the last moments of my life. You can be very sure of that. To me you are something I cannot say in words, that is how good you are. You can believe me. God? It is thanks to you that I had a beautiful life before, that I was spoiled, that I had lovely things that others didn't have. God? After this there is only one thing I want to ask of you: Make my parents come back, my poor parents, protect them (even more than me) so that I can see them again as soon as possible, let them live again one more time. Oh! I can say that I had such a wonderful mama and such a good daddy! I have such great faith in you that I thank you in advance."

Liliane Gerenstein, her brother Maurice, and the other forty-two children of Izieu were all deported and assassinated. The good have not always been rewarded and the bad have not always been punished.

In 1946, it was Mr. Lavoille, not a lawyer but the principal of the middle school of Belley, who with rare lucidity summarized the significance of this roundup and defined the specific characteristics of crimes against humanity:

"This drama was one of the most harrowing of the oppression; one of the most hateful and hideous crimes of the regime that, for five years, subjugated and tortured Europe; not merely one of the atrocities committed in the unleashing of the madness of wartime or in the frenzy of battle; but an act of hatred and cold violence, carefully thought through, methodical, and established as a doctrine of order and government."

This, I think, is the moment to pay homage to those women who have been most militant, on the one hand to see that justice is done and that the one responsible for the annihilation of their children does not remain unpunished; on the other hand to see that the memory of their children is kept alive. I am speaking of Madame Halaunbrenner and Madame Benguigui. You have seen them and you have heard them; they are both eighty-three years old; they are tired, very, very tired; they are ten years older than the executioner of their children: each mother had three children. They, as well as

Gilles Sadowski

Joseph and Henri Goldberg

other parents of children of Izieu, have been endlessly tormented ever since that April morning of 1944, when their children disappeared. Barbie has never suffered and will never suffer what these mothers of Izieu will continue to endure until their last breaths.

And yet, these mothers of Izieu have raised their heroism to the level of their children's tragedy. Sixteen years ago, when a German woman introduced herself to them and suggested they act together with her, in great risk, to obstruct Barbie's impunity, they answered "Here!" And, at the time, they were the only ones to do so despite their age and their health.

Inspired by their desire for justice, these mothers expressed themselves not with simple words alone but with extreme actions: going on a hunger strike on the steps of the Palace of Justice of Munich; rallying and chaining themselves in La Paz at an altitude of 13,123 feet in front of Barbie's office. They dared to do what so many others were not inclined to even attempt. Thus, they echoed the declaration by the Three Great Powers of October 30, 1943 which confirmed that "the allied powers shall pursue war criminals to the farthest corners of the earth and shall bring them back to the accusers so that justice will be done."

Through their valiant actions they have reached out across time to their children. They have helped to bring back the children of Izieu into the light of memory, to have them and all the other children of Izieu become a symbol of the Jewish youth martyred in France at an accursed time when, for the Gestapo, the fact of being a Jewish child would condemn you to death with greater certainty than any act of resistance. Mr. President, Gentlemen of the Court, Ladies and Gentlemen of the Jury, ever since April 6, 1944 these mothers have been waiting for Barbie, who seized their children hidden in a little French village at the other end of the world, for Barbie, brought back from the other end of the world, from the Cordillera in the Andes where he had tried to flee forever from the consequences of his acts, for Barbie, who has never renounced any of his Nazi convictions and has expressed no remorse whatsoever, for Barbie to be condemned to the sentence that the gravity of his crimes will call for, in accordance with the closing arguments of the Prosecutor that you will hear.

The Halaunbrenner Family. Far left child: Claudine. Far right children: Mina and Léon.

Maurice and Liliane Gerenstein. Right:
A letter to God from Liliane Gerenstein.

Isidore Kargeman

Charles Weltner

Alice Luzgart

Fortunée Benguigui and Beate Klarsfeld in Munich, Germany, September 13, 1971, in front of the Palace of Justice, to call for the reopening of the case against Barbie.

Ita-Rosa Halaunbrenner and Beate Klarsfeld in La Paz, Bolivia, March 6, 1972, chained in front of Barbie's office.

Fortunée Benguigui and Ita-Rosa Halaunbrenner in Izieu, France, April, 1987,
just before the third trial in Lyon, where they gave their heartbreaking testimonies.
Fortunée Benguigui died in December 1987, on the day that she was awarded the
Legion of Honor; Ita-Rosa Halaunbrenner died on May 4, 1988, and Léa Feldblum
(not pictured) died on April 9, 1989.

Mᵐᵉ **Benguigui-Chouraki**

Drawings by Plantu
made during the testimonies.

ABOUT THE AUTHOR

Attorney, author and leading historian on the fate of the Jews in France during the Second World War, Serge Klarsfeld has fought relentlessly to bring Nazi officials to justice. Born in Bucharest in 1935, Serge Klarsfeld, like Georgy, was also eight years old when his home was raided by the Gestapo. While Serge, his mother and sister escaped by hiding in a closet, his father was arrested and deported to Auschwitz where he was murdered.

Klarsfeld and his wife, Beate, first captured global attention at a political rally in 1967 when they confronted the chancellor of West Germany, Kurt-Georg Kiesinger, a former propaganda officer for Hitler. Since then Klarsfeld has tirelessly devoted himself to many legal cases against Nazi war criminals who operated in France. The Klarsfelds's most famous case was their role in the prosecution of Klaus Barbie, chief of the Lyon Gestapo and known as the notorious "Butcher of Lyon." Barbie, responsible for sending 7,000 Jews to death camps and the murder of 4,000 non-Jews, was dis-covered by Klarsfeld living comfortably in Bolivia in 1972. The Klarsfelds dedicated 10 years to research and a campaign for justice that resulted in a life-sentence for Barbie in the early '80s. Klarsfeld played an integral role in bringing a number of high-ranking officers of the Vichy government to justice including French wartime militia chief Paul Touvier and Vichy police official Maurice Papon.

Through years of painstaking research, Klarsfeld has created several documents that reveal the appalling reality of the Holocaust, including *French Children of the Holocaust: A Memorial*.

Serge Klarsfeld is Graduate of Superior Studies in History at the Sorbonne, and Graduate of the Institute of Political Science of Paris. He is also a Docteur des Lettres and lawyer at the Court of Appeal in Paris. In September 2000, Klarsfeld was named Officer of the Legion of Honor, France's highest award. President Jacques Chirac praised him as "a man who is deeply committed to justice, a tireless human rights advocate."

This publication is dedicated to Ita-Rosa Halaunbrenner and Fortunée Benguigui, two mothers of the children of Izieu. One is Ashkenazi, the other is Sephardic. Through their courage they joined the legend of Jewish mothers. Their support of Beate Klarsfeld in Germany, right up until Bolivia in 1971 and 1972 and later at the trial of Barbie in 1987, demonstrates how the murder of their children led them to an exemplary action of justice and memory.

SERGE KLARSFELD